Title of the Book

"Decisions Powered by Data: A Practical Guide for Organizations"

By
Ms. Manpreet Kaur
Assistant-Professor
Chandigarh University,
Gharuan, Mohali

Table of Contents

Introduction

- **Overview of Data-Driven Decision-Making**
    - Importance of data in modern organizations
    - Benefits of adopting a data-driven culture

Chapter 1: Understanding Data

- Types of Data
    - Quantitative vs. Qualitative
    - Structured vs. Unstructured
- Data Sources
    - Internal vs. External sources
    - Primary vs. Secondary data

Chapter 2: Data Collection and Management

- Strategies for Effective Data Collection
    - Surveys, interviews, and observational methods
- Data Storage and Management
    - Database systems and data warehouses
    - Best practices for data governance and security

Chapter 3: Data Analysis Techniques

- Descriptive Analysis
- Diagnostic Analysis
- Predictive Analysis
- Prescriptive Analysis
- Tools and Software for Data Analysis

Chapter 4: Making Data-Driven Decisions

- Frameworks for Decision-Making
    - The OODA Loop (Observe, Orient, Decide, Act)
    - SWOT Analysis with a Data Perspective
- Integrating Data Insights into Strategic Planning

Chapter 5: Case Studies

- Successful Implementations
    - Organizations that thrived using data-driven strategies
- Lessons Learned from Failures
    - Common pitfalls and how to avoid them

Chapter 6: Building a Data-Driven Culture

- Importance of Leadership Support
- Training and Development for Employees
- Fostering Collaboration between Departments

Chapter 7: Ethical Considerations in Data Use

- Privacy Concerns and Data Ethics
- Bias in Data and Decision-Making
- Regulatory Compliance

Chapter 8: Future Trends in Data-Driven Decision-Making

- Emerging Technologies (AI, ML, Big Data)
- The Role of Data in Sustainable Practices
- Predictions for the Future of Data in Organizations

Conclusion

- Summary of Key Takeaways
- Call to Action for Organizations

Additional Components

- **Appendices**:
    - Glossary of Terms
    - Recommended Tools and Resources
- **References and Further Reading**

Introduction

In today's fast-paced and complex business environment, the ability to make informed decisions can mean the difference between success and failure. As organizations navigate unprecedented challenges and opportunities, the reliance on data has become paramount. Data-driven decision-making (DDDM) empowers leaders and teams to base their strategies on factual insights rather than intuition or anecdotal evidence.

Overview of Data-Driven Decision-Making

Data-driven decision-making refers to the practice of collecting and analyzing data to guide business choices and strategies. It encompasses a wide range of methodologies and techniques that enable organizations to turn raw data into actionable insights. From customer behaviour patterns to operational efficiencies, the insights gleaned from data can illuminate pathways to innovation, growth, and improved performance.

In recent years, advancements in technology have revolutionized the way organizations gather, store, and analyze data. With the rise of big data analytics, artificial intelligence (AI), and machine learning (ML), businesses can now process vast amounts of information at unprecedented speeds. This evolution has made it essential for organizations to integrate data into their decision-making processes, allowing them to stay competitive in an increasingly data-centric world.

Importance of Data in Modern Organizations

The significance of data in modern organizations cannot be overstated. Data serves as a critical asset that informs every aspect of a business, from marketing strategies to operational processes. By leveraging data, organizations can:

- **Enhance Customer Understanding**: Analyzing customer data helps businesses identify preferences, behaviours, and trends, enabling them to tailor products and services to meet customer needs effectively.
- **Optimize Operations**: Data analysis can reveal inefficiencies and bottlenecks within operations, allowing organizations to streamline processes, reduce costs, and improve productivity.
- **Drive Innovation**: Insights derived from data can inspire new ideas, products, and services, fostering a culture of innovation that keeps organizations ahead of their competitors.
- **Mitigate Risks**: By analyzing historical data and market trends, organizations can identify potential risks and make informed decisions to mitigate them, enhancing overall resilience.

Benefits of Adopting a Data-Driven Culture

Embracing a data-driven culture is not just about utilizing data; it's about fostering an organizational mindset that values and prioritizes data in every decision. The benefits of adopting such a culture include:

- **Improved Decision-Making**: When decisions are based on data rather than gut feelings, organizations can reduce bias and make more accurate predictions about future outcomes.
- **Enhanced Accountability**: A data-driven approach encourages transparency and accountability, as decisions can be traced back to concrete evidence and insights.
- **Increased Agility**: Organizations that prioritize data can respond more swiftly to market changes and customer demands, enabling them to capitalize on emerging opportunities.
- **Empowered Employees**: By providing employees with access to data and the tools to analyze it, organizations can cultivate a workforce that is engaged, informed, and capable of contributing to strategic discussions.

In conclusion, as organizations strive to thrive in an ever-evolving landscape, embracing data-driven decision-making is essential. This book will explore the principles, techniques, and best practices of DDDM, offering practical guidance for organizations looking to harness the power of data in their decision-making processes. Through this journey, we will uncover how a commitment to data can transform not only decisions but the very fabric of organizational culture.

Chapter 1: Understanding Data

In a data-driven world, understanding the types of data and their sources is fundamental to effective decision-making. Data can take many forms, each offering unique insights and implications for analysis. This chapter will explore the various types of data, their characteristics, and the sources from which they can be obtained.

Types of Data

Data can be categorized in several ways, each serving a different purpose in analysis and decision-making. Two primary distinctions are quantitative vs. qualitative data and structured vs. unstructured data.

Quantitative vs. Qualitative

- **Quantitative Data**: This type of data is numerical and can be measured or counted. It is often used to analyze trends, patterns, and relationships through statistical methods. Examples include sales figures, customer demographics, and performance metrics. Quantitative data allows organizations to quantify their performance and make data-driven predictions.
    - **Characteristics**:
        - Measurable: Can be expressed in numbers.
        - Objective: Provides a clear and unbiased view of data.

- Suitable for statistical analysis: Facilitates hypothesis testing and predictive modeling.
- **Qualitative Data**: In contrast, qualitative data is descriptive and subjective. It provides insights into the underlying motivations, opinions, and experiences of individuals. This type of data is often collected through interviews, focus groups, and open-ended survey questions. Qualitative data can help organizations understand the context behind the numbers and uncover rich narratives.
  - **Characteristics**:
    - Descriptive: Captures thoughts, feelings, and experiences.
    - Subjective: Interpretation can vary based on individual perspectives.
    - Ideal for exploratory analysis: Helps generate hypotheses and identify themes.

Structured vs. Unstructured

Data can also be classified as structured or unstructured, reflecting its format and organization.

- **Structured Data**: This type of data is organized in a predefined format, making it easily searchable and analyzable. Structured data is typically stored in relational databases and spreadsheets, where it can be efficiently processed using standard query languages. Examples include customer names, transaction records, and inventory levels.
  - **Characteristics**:
    - Highly organized: Follows a specific schema or model.
    - Easily analyzed: Can be processed using traditional data analysis tools.
    - High accuracy: Less prone to errors and inconsistencies.

- **Unstructured Data**: Unstructured data lacks a predefined format, making it more challenging to analyze. It includes text documents, emails, social media posts, images, and videos. Unstructured data can provide valuable insights but often requires advanced analytical techniques, such as natural language processing (NLP) or machine learning, to extract meaningful information.
    - **Characteristics**:
        - Disorganized: Does not follow a specific format or structure.
        - Complex to analyze: Requires advanced tools and techniques.
        - Rich in insights: Can uncover nuanced patterns and trends.

Data Sources

Understanding where data comes from is equally important as understanding its types. Data sources can be classified into internal and external sources, as well as primary and secondary data.

Internal vs. External Sources

- **Internal Sources**: These are data generated within the organization. Internal sources can include sales records, customer databases, employee performance evaluations, and financial reports. Leveraging internal data allows organizations to gain insights into their operations, performance, and customer interactions.
    - **Advantages**:
        - Familiarity: Organizations have control over the data collection process.

- Relevance: Internal data is often closely aligned with business goals and objectives.
            - Cost-effective: Reduces the need for external data acquisition.
- **External Sources**: External data comes from outside the organization and can provide valuable context and benchmarks. Examples include market research reports, social media analytics, industry publications, and government databases. External sources can help organizations understand market trends, competitive dynamics, and consumer behavior.
    - **Advantages**:
        - Broader perspective: Offers insights beyond the organization's own data.
        - Competitive intelligence: Provides information about industry trends and competitor activities.
        - Access to diverse data: Expands the analytical scope.

Primary vs. Secondary Data

- **Primary Data**: This data is collected directly from the source for a specific research purpose. Organizations can gather primary data through surveys, interviews, experiments, or observations. While primary data collection can be resource-intensive, it offers tailored insights that directly address the organization's needs.
    - **Advantages**:
        - Specificity: Tailored to the organization's particular research questions.
        - Control over data quality: Organizations can ensure the reliability and validity of the data.

- **Secondary Data**: Secondary data is collected by someone else for a different purpose but can still be relevant to an organization's research needs. This includes published research studies, statistical databases, and reports from governmental and non-governmental organizations. Secondary data can be a cost-effective way to access a wealth of information.
    - **Advantages**:
        - Cost-efficient: Often less expensive than primary data collection.
        - Time-saving: Provides immediate access to existing information.

Conclusion

Understanding the types of data and their sources is crucial for organizations looking to make informed decisions. By effectively leveraging quantitative, qualitative, structured, and unstructured data, and by identifying the right sources, organizations can gain insights that drive strategy, enhance performance, and foster innovation. As we continue through this book, we will delve deeper into how to collect, analyze, and apply these insights to make data-driven decisions that propel organizations forward.

Chapter 2: Data Collection and Management

Once an organization understands the types of data and their sources, the next critical step is collecting and managing that data effectively. Proper data collection and management are vital for ensuring the quality, accessibility, and security of data. This chapter will explore strategies for effective data collection, as well as the systems and best practices for data storage and management.

Strategies for Effective Data Collection

Effective data collection involves using various methods to gather information that is reliable, relevant, and representative. The choice of method often depends on the research objectives, the nature of the data, and the resources available. Common strategies include surveys, interviews, and observational methods.

Surveys

Surveys are a popular method for collecting quantitative data from a large number of respondents. They can be administered through various formats, including online questionnaires, telephone interviews, or face-to-face interactions. Surveys typically consist of structured questions, allowing for easy analysis of responses.

- **Advantages**:

- Cost-effective: Online surveys, in particular, can reach a large audience at a low cost.
- Quick data collection: Surveys can be distributed and completed in a relatively short timeframe.
- Quantifiable results: Provides numerical data that can be statistically analyzed.

- **Considerations**:
    - Question design: Poorly worded questions can lead to biased responses.
    - Response rates: Ensuring a high response rate is crucial for the validity of the results.

Interviews

Interviews provide a qualitative approach to data collection, allowing for in-depth exploration of respondents' thoughts and experiences. They can be structured, semi-structured, or unstructured, depending on the level of flexibility desired in the conversation.

- **Advantages**:
    - Depth of insight: Interviews allow for deeper exploration of topics and can uncover rich narratives.
    - Flexibility: Interviewers can adapt their questions based on the flow of the conversation.
- **Considerations**:
    - Time-consuming: Interviews can take considerable time to conduct and analyze.
    - Interviewer bias: The interviewer's presence and questions can influence responses.

Observational Methods

Observational methods involve collecting data by observing subjects in their natural environment. This technique is particularly useful in understanding behaviors, processes, and interactions.

- **Advantages**:
    - Real-time insights: Observations can provide immediate, firsthand information.
    - Contextual understanding: This method captures the context in which behaviors occur.
- **Considerations**:
    - Subjectivity: Observations may be influenced by the observer's biases and interpretations.
    - Limited scalability: Observing a large number of subjects can be impractical.

Data Storage and Management

Once data is collected, it must be stored and managed effectively to ensure it remains accessible, secure, and usable. Organizations rely on various database systems and data warehouses to store data, as well as best practices for data governance and security.

Database Systems and Data Warehouses

- **Database Systems**: These are structured collections of data that allow for easy storage, retrieval, and manipulation. Relational databases (e.g., MySQL, PostgreSQL) store data in tables with predefined relationships, while NoSQL databases (e.g., MongoDB, Cassandra) are designed to handle unstructured or semi-structured data.

- **Advantages**:
  - Scalability: Many database systems can handle large volumes of data.
  - Flexibility: NoSQL databases can accommodate various data types and structures.

- **Data Warehouses**: A data warehouse is a centralized repository designed for analysis and reporting. It consolidates data from multiple sources, providing a holistic view of an organization's data. Data warehouses typically employ ETL (Extract, Transform, Load) processes to prepare data for analysis.

  - **Advantages**:
    - Improved analytics: Data warehouses facilitate complex queries and reporting.
    - Historical data retention: They enable organizations to analyze trends over time.

Best Practices for Data Governance and Security

Effective data management requires robust governance and security measures to protect sensitive information and ensure data quality. Organizations should adopt the following best practices:

- **Data Governance**: Establishing a data governance framework ensures that data is accurate, consistent, and compliant with regulations. This includes defining data ownership, quality standards, and policies for data access and usage.
  - **Key Components**:

- Data stewardship: Assigning responsibility for data quality and management.
- Data policies: Developing guidelines for data usage, retention, and disposal.

- **Data Security**: Protecting data from unauthorized access, breaches, and loss is crucial for maintaining trust and compliance. Organizations should implement strong security measures, such as encryption, access controls, and regular audits.
  - **Key Components**:
    - User authentication: Implementing strong password policies and multi-factor authentication.
    - Data backup: Regularly backing up data to prevent loss in case of system failures or breaches.

Conclusion

Effective data collection and management are foundational to a successful data-driven strategy. By employing appropriate data collection methods and leveraging robust storage systems, organizations can ensure that they gather high-quality data that is accessible and secure. As we continue this journey through the book, we will explore data analysis techniques that will enable organizations to extract valuable insights from their data, driving informed decision-making and strategic growth.

Chapter 3: Data Analysis Techniques

Data analysis is a critical step in the data-driven decision-making process. By analyzing data, organizations can extract meaningful insights, identify trends, and make informed decisions that drive success. This chapter explores four fundamental types of data analysis techniques—descriptive, diagnostic, predictive, and prescriptive—and highlights various tools and software that can aid in the analysis process.

Descriptive Analysis

Descriptive analysis provides a summary of historical data, helping organizations understand what has happened in the past. This technique involves the use of statistical measures to describe and interpret data sets. Common methods of descriptive analysis include mean, median, mode, standard deviation, and data visualization techniques such as charts and graphs.

- **Purpose**:
    - To provide a clear overview of past events, behaviors, or performance metrics.
- **Applications**:
    - Sales performance analysis: Understanding sales trends over specific periods.
    - Customer demographics: Analyzing customer profiles to inform marketing strategies.

- **Example**:
    - A retail company analyzes its sales data from the last year to determine the average monthly revenue and identify peak sales periods.

Diagnostic Analysis

While descriptive analysis answers the question of what happened, diagnostic analysis seeks to understand why it happened. This technique involves examining data to identify relationships, correlations, and patterns that explain past events. Diagnostic analysis often uses methods such as data mining, correlation analysis, and root cause analysis.

- **Purpose**:
    - To investigate and uncover the underlying causes of trends or anomalies in data.
- **Applications**:
    - Performance issues: Identifying factors contributing to declining sales or customer satisfaction.
    - Marketing effectiveness: Evaluating the impact of marketing campaigns on customer behavior.
- **Example**:
    - An organization discovers that a drop in customer satisfaction correlates with longer wait times in customer service, prompting an investigation into staffing levels and operational processes.

Predictive Analysis

Predictive analysis utilizes historical data and statistical algorithms to forecast future outcomes. This technique is particularly valuable for organizations seeking to anticipate trends and make proactive decisions. Predictive analysis often employs machine learning models and regression analysis to identify patterns that can inform future predictions.

- **Purpose**:
    - To forecast potential future events based on historical data trends.
- **Applications**:
    - Sales forecasting: Predicting future sales based on past performance and market conditions.
    - Customer behavior prediction: Anticipating customer needs and preferences for targeted marketing.
- **Example**:
    - A financial institution uses predictive modeling to assess the likelihood of loan defaults based on applicant credit scores and historical repayment patterns.

Prescriptive Analysis

Prescriptive analysis goes a step further by recommending actions based on predictive insights. This technique combines data analysis, business rules, and optimization algorithms to suggest the best course of action to achieve desired outcomes. Prescriptive analysis is valuable for decision-making in complex scenarios where multiple variables and constraints must be considered.

- **Purpose**:
    - To provide actionable recommendations for optimal decision-making.

- **Applications**:
    - Inventory management: Optimizing stock levels to minimize costs while meeting customer demand.
    - Resource allocation: Determining the best allocation of resources across projects for maximum impact.
- **Example**:
    - An e-commerce company employs prescriptive analysis to determine the ideal pricing strategy for products based on competitor pricing, demand forecasts, and customer behavior.

Tools and Software for Data Analysis

To effectively perform data analysis, organizations can leverage a variety of tools and software designed to support different analytical techniques. These tools can enhance productivity, accuracy, and collaboration among teams. Some popular data analysis tools include:

- **Microsoft Excel**: A widely used tool for basic data analysis and visualization, Excel offers functions for statistical analysis, pivot tables, and charting capabilities.
- **Tableau**: A powerful data visualization tool that enables users to create interactive and shareable dashboards, helping to visualize complex data sets in an accessible format.
- **R and Python**: Programming languages that provide extensive libraries for statistical analysis, machine learning, and data visualization, making them ideal for advanced analytics.
- **Power BI**: A business analytics tool by Microsoft that enables users to create reports and dashboards, providing insights into data through visualizations and interactive features.

- **SAS**: A software suite for advanced analytics, business intelligence, and data management, SAS is known for its powerful statistical capabilities and predictive modeling.
- **Google Analytics**: A web analytics tool that tracks and reports website traffic, providing insights into user behavior and the effectiveness of digital marketing efforts.

Conclusion

Data analysis techniques are essential for transforming raw data into actionable insights that drive informed decision-making. By employing descriptive, diagnostic, predictive, and prescriptive analysis methods, organizations can understand past performance, uncover underlying causes, forecast future outcomes, and recommend optimal actions. The right tools and software further empower organizations to streamline the analysis process, enabling them to leverage data for strategic growth and competitive advantage. In the next chapter, we will explore how to make data-driven decisions based on these analytical insights.

Chapter 4: Making Data-Driven Decisions

Data-driven decision-making is a systematic approach that empowers organizations to leverage data insights for strategic planning and operational effectiveness. This chapter explores frameworks for effective decision-making, such as the OODA Loop and SWOT analysis, and discusses how to integrate data insights into strategic planning processes.

Frameworks for Decision-Making

Frameworks provide structured methodologies that guide decision-makers in analyzing data and determining the best course of action. Two widely recognized frameworks are the OODA Loop and SWOT analysis, both of which can be enhanced with a data perspective.

The OODA Loop (Observe, Orient, Decide, Act)

The OODA Loop is a decision-making framework developed by military strategist John Boyd. It consists of four stages: Observe, Orient, Decide, and Act. This iterative process allows organizations to adapt quickly to changing circumstances by continuously gathering data and refining their strategies.

1. **Observe**: In this initial stage, organizations collect data from various sources, including internal metrics, market research, and customer feedback. The focus is on gathering relevant information that can inform the decision-making process.
2. **Orient**: During the orientation phase, organizations analyze the collected data to identify patterns, trends, and insights. This stage involves synthesizing information and considering external factors, such as competition and market dynamics, to gain a comprehensive understanding of the situation.
3. **Decide**: Based on the insights gained during the orientation phase, decision-makers evaluate potential options and select the best course of action. This stage may involve predictive analysis to assess the likely outcomes of each option.
4. **Act**: The final phase involves implementing the chosen decision. After taking action, organizations should continue to monitor outcomes and gather feedback to inform future iterations of the OODA Loop.

Benefits of the OODA Loop:

- **Agility**: The iterative nature of the OODA Loop allows organizations to adapt to changes quickly.
- **Continuous improvement**: Regularly revisiting each phase helps refine decision-making processes over time.
- **Data-driven insights**: Each stage emphasizes the importance of using data to inform decisions.

SWOT Analysis with a Data Perspective

SWOT analysis is a strategic planning tool that helps organizations identify their strengths, weaknesses, opportunities, and threats. By integrating a data perspective, organizations can enhance the effectiveness of SWOT analysis and ensure that decisions are informed by factual insights.

1. **Strengths**: Identify internal attributes that provide a competitive advantage. Use data to quantify strengths, such as market share, customer loyalty metrics, or operational efficiencies.
2. **Weaknesses**: Assess internal limitations or areas for improvement. Data can highlight weaknesses in performance metrics, customer satisfaction scores, or operational bottlenecks.
3. **Opportunities**: Explore external factors that could be leveraged for growth. Analyze market trends, customer behavior data, and competitive intelligence to identify emerging opportunities.
4. **Threats**: Evaluate external challenges that could impact the organization. Use data to monitor competitor actions, market shifts, and economic indicators to assess potential threats.

Benefits of SWOT Analysis with a Data Perspective:

- **Informed decision-making**: Data-driven insights provide a factual basis for assessing strengths, weaknesses, opportunities, and threats.
- **Holistic view**: Integrating data ensures that both internal and external factors are considered in strategic planning.

- **Prioritized actions**: Quantifying strengths and weaknesses helps organizations focus on the most impactful areas for improvement and growth.

Integrating Data Insights into Strategic Planning

Integrating data insights into strategic planning is essential for aligning organizational goals with actionable data. Here are some steps organizations can take to ensure that data-driven insights are effectively integrated into their strategic planning processes:

1. **Establish clear objectives**: Define specific, measurable, achievable, relevant, and time-bound (SMART) objectives that align with organizational goals. Ensure that these objectives are informed by data insights.
2. **Create a data-driven culture**: Foster a culture that values data in decision-making. Encourage teams to rely on data insights when developing strategies and initiatives, and provide training to enhance data literacy across the organization.
3. **Utilize analytics tools**: Implement analytics tools and software that facilitate data analysis and visualization. Ensure that decision-makers have access to relevant dashboards and reports that provide real-time insights into performance metrics.
4. **Incorporate stakeholder input**: Involve key stakeholders in the strategic planning process to ensure diverse perspectives are considered. Use data to facilitate discussions and align stakeholders on strategic priorities.
5. **Monitor progress**: Regularly track and analyze key performance indicators (KPIs) to assess the effectiveness of strategies. Use insights from ongoing data analysis to adjust plans and make informed decisions as needed.

6. **Encourage feedback loops**: Establish mechanisms for collecting feedback on strategic initiatives. Use this feedback, combined with data insights, to refine strategies and enhance future decision-making processes.

Conclusion

Making data-driven decisions is essential for organizations seeking to thrive in a competitive landscape. By employing frameworks like the OODA Loop and SWOT analysis, organizations can structure their decision-making processes to leverage data insights effectively. Integrating data into strategic planning not only enhances the quality of decisions but also fosters a culture of continuous improvement and agility. In the following chapters, we will explore case studies and practical applications that illustrate successful data-driven decision-making in various organizational contexts.

Chapter 5: Case Studies

Case studies provide valuable insights into real-world applications of data-driven decision-making, showcasing both successful implementations and lessons learned from failures. This chapter highlights organizations that have thrived using data-driven strategies and examines common pitfalls that can hinder success, offering guidance on how to avoid them.

Successful Implementations

Organizations across various industries have successfully leveraged data-driven strategies to enhance performance, drive innovation, and achieve competitive advantage. Here are a few notable examples:

1. Amazon

Overview: As one of the world's largest e-commerce platforms, Amazon has made data-driven decision-making a core part of its business strategy.

Implementation: Amazon employs sophisticated algorithms and data analytics to personalize customer experiences. By analyzing user behavior, purchase history, and browsing patterns, the company can recommend products tailored to individual preferences.

Outcome: This approach has led to increased customer satisfaction and loyalty, significantly boosting sales. Amazon's recommendation engine reportedly accounts for 35% of its total sales.

Key Takeaway: Personalization through data analytics can drive customer engagement and sales, emphasizing the importance of understanding consumer behavior.

2. Netflix

Overview: Netflix is a leading streaming service that has successfully harnessed data to revolutionize content creation and customer experience.

Implementation: The company uses data analytics to monitor viewer preferences, behaviors, and trends. By analyzing this data, Netflix can determine which shows to produce, how to market them, and what content to recommend to individual users.

Outcome: This data-driven approach has resulted in a significant reduction in content development risks, leading to successful original programming such as "Stranger Things" and "The Crown." As a result, Netflix has seen substantial subscriber growth and retention.

Key Takeaway: Data analytics can inform content development strategies, helping organizations create products that resonate with their target audience.

3. Target

Overview: Target, a major retail corporation, has effectively utilized data analytics to enhance customer targeting and marketing strategies.

Implementation: By analyzing purchasing patterns and demographic data, Target can identify specific customer segments and tailor marketing campaigns accordingly. One notable example involved identifying expectant mothers and providing personalized offers and recommendations based on their needs.

Outcome: This strategy not only increased sales among targeted customer segments but also fostered customer loyalty and improved brand perception.

Key Takeaway: Leveraging data to understand customer segments enables organizations to create targeted marketing strategies that resonate with consumers.

Lessons Learned from Failures

While many organizations have successfully implemented data-driven strategies, others have encountered challenges and setbacks. Understanding these failures can help prevent similar pitfalls in future initiatives. Here are some common lessons learned from failures in data-driven decision-making:

1. Blockbuster's Missed Opportunity

Overview: Once a dominant player in the video rental industry, Blockbuster failed to adapt to the rise of digital streaming and on-demand content.

Failure Point: Blockbuster had access to vast amounts of customer data but did not leverage it effectively. The company underestimated the potential of online streaming, ultimately allowing competitors like Netflix to gain a foothold in the market.

Lesson Learned: Organizations must remain agile and responsive to changing market dynamics. Relying on historical success can blind organizations to emerging trends and opportunities.

2. Target's Predictive Analytics Blunder

Overview: Target's use of predictive analytics to identify customer segments led to a public relations crisis in 2012.

Failure Point: The company accurately identified pregnant customers through purchasing patterns but faced backlash when it sent targeted advertisements to a teenage girl, revealing her pregnancy before she had informed her family.

Lesson Learned: While data-driven insights can provide valuable information, organizations must approach sensitive topics with caution. Ethical considerations and customer privacy should always guide data usage.

3. Yahoo's Data Overload

Overview: Yahoo struggled to harness the potential of its vast data resources, ultimately leading to its decline as a tech giant.

Failure Point: Despite having access to significant amounts of user data, Yahoo failed to create a cohesive data strategy. The organization lacked a clear vision for how to leverage data for product development and marketing.

Lesson Learned: Having access to data is not enough; organizations must develop a clear strategy for how to analyze and utilize that data effectively. Aligning data initiatives with business goals is crucial for success.

Conclusion

The case studies presented in this chapter illustrate the transformative power of data-driven decision-making in diverse organizations. Success stories like Amazon, Netflix, and Target highlight the potential for leveraging data to enhance customer experiences and drive business growth. Conversely, lessons from failures such as Blockbuster, Target, and Yahoo underscore the importance of agility, ethical considerations, and strategic alignment in data initiatives. By learning from both successes and failures, organizations can navigate the complexities of data-driven decision-making and achieve their strategic objectives. In the next chapter, we will explore practical steps for implementing a data-driven culture within organizations.

Chapter 6: Building a Data-Driven Culture

Creating a data-driven culture is essential for organizations seeking to leverage data effectively in their decision-making processes. A robust data culture empowers employees to use data confidently and fosters an environment where data-driven insights are prioritized. This chapter explores the importance of leadership support, the role of training and development for employees, and strategies for fostering collaboration between departments.

Importance of Leadership Support

Leadership plays a crucial role in establishing and nurturing a data-driven culture within an organization. Leaders set the tone and expectations for how data is perceived and used across all levels of the organization.

1. **Vision and Commitment**: Leaders must articulate a clear vision for data-driven decision-making and demonstrate a commitment to leveraging data in strategic planning and daily operations. This commitment sends a message that data is valued and integral to the organization's success.

2. **Resource Allocation**: Effective leaders allocate resources—both financial and human—toward data initiatives. This may include investing in data analytics tools, hiring data scientists, and providing access to training programs for employees.
3. **Role Modeling**: Leaders should lead by example, using data to inform their own decisions and sharing data-driven insights with their teams. By modeling data-driven behavior, leaders encourage employees to adopt similar practices.
4. **Encouraging Risk-Taking**: A culture that embraces experimentation and innovation encourages employees to explore new data-driven initiatives without the fear of failure. Leaders should promote a mindset that values learning from data and adapting based on insights.

Training and Development for Employees

To build a data-driven culture, organizations must invest in the training and development of their employees. Empowering employees with the skills and knowledge to work with data is essential for maximizing the value of data-driven decision-making.

1. **Data Literacy Programs**: Implementing data literacy programs helps employees at all levels understand how to read, interpret, and analyze data. These programs should cover basic statistical concepts, data visualization techniques, and the use of analytics tools.
2. **Role-Specific Training**: Tailor training programs to meet the specific needs of different roles within the organization. For example, sales teams may benefit from training on customer analytics, while marketing teams might focus on data-driven campaign strategies.

3. **Continuous Learning**: Encourage a culture of continuous learning by offering ongoing training opportunities, workshops, and access to online courses. This commitment to professional development helps employees stay updated on the latest data trends and technologies.
4. **Mentorship and Collaboration**: Foster mentorship opportunities where experienced data professionals can guide and support less experienced employees. Encourage collaboration between teams to share knowledge and best practices related to data usage.

Fostering Collaboration between Departments

Collaboration between departments is critical for building a cohesive data-driven culture. Data insights often span multiple areas of the organization, and cross-departmental collaboration can enhance the quality and applicability of data-driven decisions.

1. **Establish Cross-Functional Teams**: Create cross-functional teams that bring together individuals from various departments, such as marketing, sales, finance, and operations. These teams can work together on data projects, share insights, and identify opportunities for collaboration.
2. **Shared Goals and Metrics**: Align departmental goals with overarching organizational objectives to ensure that all teams are working toward common data-driven outcomes. Establish shared performance metrics that encourage departments to collaborate and support each other.
3. **Communication and Information Sharing**: Foster open communication and information sharing among departments. Implement collaboration tools and platforms that facilitate data sharing and allow teams to access relevant data insights easily.

4. **Celebrate Successes**: Recognize and celebrate successful data-driven initiatives that result from cross-departmental collaboration. Acknowledging these achievements reinforces the importance of working together and encourages continued collaboration.

Conclusion

Building a data-driven culture is a multifaceted endeavour that requires commitment and effort from all levels of the organization. Leadership support is vital in establishing a clear vision and allocating resources for data initiatives. Training and development for employees empower individuals to harness the power of data effectively while fostering collaboration between departments enhances the overall impact of data-driven decision-making. As organizations cultivate a strong data-driven culture, they position themselves to adapt to changing market dynamics, innovate more effectively, and drive sustainable growth. In the following chapters, we will explore future trends in data-driven decision-making and the role of emerging technologies in shaping the data landscape.

Chapter 7: Ethical Considerations in Data Use

As organizations increasingly rely on data-driven decision-making, ethical considerations become paramount. This chapter explores the critical issues surrounding privacy concerns, bias in data and decision-making, and the importance of regulatory compliance. Addressing these ethical challenges is essential for building trust with stakeholders and ensuring responsible data use.

Privacy Concerns and Data Ethics

The collection and use of data raise significant privacy concerns, as organizations must navigate the fine line between leveraging data for insights and respecting individuals' privacy rights.

1. **Informed Consent**: Organizations should prioritize obtaining informed consent from individuals before collecting their data. This involves clearly communicating how data will be used, stored, and shared, allowing individuals to make informed decisions about their data.

2. **Data Minimization**: Practicing data minimization involves collecting only the data necessary for a specific purpose. Organizations should avoid gathering excessive or irrelevant data that could compromise privacy and increase the risk of misuse.
3. **Anonymization and De-identification**: To protect individual privacy, organizations should consider anonymizing or de-identifying data whenever possible. This practice helps reduce the risk of identifying individuals from aggregated data sets.
4. **Transparency**: Organizations must maintain transparency in their data practices by clearly communicating their data policies to stakeholders. Providing insight into data collection methods, usage, and retention policies builds trust and accountability.
5. **Ethical Data Use Frameworks**: Organizations should adopt ethical frameworks that guide data use. These frameworks should outline principles for responsible data collection, storage, analysis, and sharing, ensuring that ethical considerations are integrated into decision-making processes.

Bias in Data and Decision-Making

Bias in data can lead to skewed insights and unfair outcomes, making it crucial for organizations to recognize and address bias in their data and decision-making processes.

1. **Understanding Bias**: Bias can arise from various sources, including data collection methods, sampling issues, and historical prejudices reflected in the data. Organizations must understand the types of bias that may exist and their potential impact on decision-making.

2. **Diverse Data Sources**: To mitigate bias, organizations should strive to use diverse data sources that represent a wide range of perspectives and experiences. This approach helps ensure that insights derived from data are more representative and inclusive.
3. **Bias Detection and Correction**: Implementing bias detection tools and techniques can help organizations identify and address biases in their data and algorithms. Regularly auditing data sets and decision-making processes is essential to ensure fairness and accuracy.
4. **Ethical AI and Machine Learning**: As organizations increasingly rely on AI and machine learning for decision-making, ethical considerations must be prioritized. Developing algorithms that are transparent and fair is critical to preventing biased outcomes that could harm marginalized groups.
5. **Promoting Accountability**: Establishing accountability mechanisms within organizations can help ensure that data-driven decisions are made with fairness and equity in mind. Organizations should encourage open discussions about potential biases and their implications.

Regulatory Compliance

Organizations must comply with various regulations governing data use and privacy to avoid legal repercussions and build trust with stakeholders.

1. **Understanding Data Regulations**: Familiarizing themselves with relevant data regulations is crucial for organizations. Key regulations include the General Data Protection Regulation (GDPR) in the European Union, the California Consumer Privacy

Act (CCPA) in the United States, and other local and international laws governing data privacy and protection.

2. **Data Protection Officers (DPOs)**: Appointing a Data Protection Officer can help organizations ensure compliance with data regulations. DPOs oversee data protection strategies, monitor compliance, and serve as points of contact for data subjects and regulatory authorities.

3. **Conducting Data Audits**: Regular data audits can help organizations assess their compliance with data regulations. These audits should evaluate data collection practices, storage methods, and security measures to identify potential gaps and areas for improvement.

4. **Incident Response Plans**: Organizations should establish incident response plans to address data breaches or compliance failures promptly. These plans should outline procedures for reporting incidents, notifying affected individuals, and mitigating potential harm.

5. **Training and Awareness**: Providing training for employees on data privacy regulations and ethical data use is essential for fostering a culture of compliance. Employees should understand their responsibilities regarding data handling and the implications of non-compliance.

Conclusion

Ethical considerations in data use are essential for organizations seeking to harness the power of data responsibly. By addressing privacy concerns, mitigating bias, and ensuring regulatory compliance, organizations can build trust with stakeholders and promote ethical data practices.

As data-driven decision-making continues to evolve, organizations must remain vigilant in prioritizing ethical considerations to ensure that data is used responsibly and equitably. In the next chapter, we will explore future trends in data-driven decision-making and the role of emerging technologies in shaping the data landscape.

Chapter 8: Future Trends in Data-Driven Decision-Making

As organizations increasingly embrace data-driven decision-making, emerging technologies and evolving practices continue to shape the data landscape. This chapter explores the impact of technologies such as artificial intelligence (AI), machine learning (ML), and big data, the role of data in sustainable practices, and predictions for the future of data use in organizations.

Emerging Technologies (AI, ML, Big Data)

The rapid advancement of technology is transforming the way organizations collect, analyze, and utilize data. Key technologies influencing data-driven decision-making include AI, ML, and big data.

1. **Artificial Intelligence (AI)**: AI encompasses a range of technologies that enable machines to perform tasks that typically require human intelligence, such as understanding natural language, recognizing patterns, and making predictions. Organizations are increasingly leveraging AI to enhance data analysis, automate processes, and gain deeper insights from their data.
    - **Applications**: AI is being used in various sectors, including finance for fraud detection, healthcare for predictive diagnostics, and marketing for customer segmentation. By automating data analysis, AI can uncover trends and insights that would be difficult for humans to identify alone.
2. **Machine Learning (ML)**: A subset of AI, ML involves algorithms that allow systems to learn from data and improve their performance over time without being explicitly programmed. ML is transforming how organizations approach data analysis and decision-making.
    - **Applications**: ML algorithms are used for predictive analytics, recommendation systems, and anomaly detection. For example, e-commerce companies use ML to analyze customer behavior and provide personalized product recommendations, leading to higher conversion rates.
3. **Big Data**: The explosion of data generated from various sources—social media, IoT devices, and online transactions—has led to the emergence of big data. This term refers to vast, complex data sets that traditional data processing applications struggle to handle.
    - **Applications**: Organizations are harnessing big data analytics to gain real-time insights, optimize operations, and improve customer experiences. Industries such

as retail, finance, and healthcare are using big data to drive innovation and enhance decision-making capabilities.

The Role of Data in Sustainable Practices

Data is becoming increasingly important in driving sustainable practices within organizations. By leveraging data insights, organizations can make informed decisions that promote environmental sustainability and social responsibility.

1. **Resource Optimization**: Organizations can use data to identify inefficiencies in resource usage, such as energy consumption, waste production, and supply chain operations. By analyzing this data, organizations can implement strategies to reduce waste, conserve resources, and improve overall sustainability.
    - **Example**: Manufacturing companies can analyze data from production processes to minimize waste and optimize energy consumption, leading to both cost savings and reduced environmental impact.
2. **Sustainable Supply Chains**: Data can help organizations build sustainable supply chains by providing insights into sourcing practices, transportation emissions, and supplier sustainability metrics. Organizations can make informed choices about suppliers and logistics to minimize their carbon footprint.
    - **Example**: Retailers can analyze data on the environmental impact of their suppliers to choose partners who align with their sustainability goals.
3. **Monitoring and Reporting**: Data analytics enables organizations to monitor and report on their sustainability efforts effectively. By tracking key performance indicators (KPIs)

related to environmental impact, organizations can assess their progress toward sustainability goals and make data-driven adjustments as needed.

- **Example**: Companies can use data to report on their carbon emissions, water usage, and waste management practices, helping them to meet regulatory requirements and communicate their sustainability efforts to stakeholders.

Predictions for the Future of Data in Organizations

As technology continues to evolve, several trends are expected to shape the future of data-driven decision-making in organizations:

1. **Increased Automation**: Organizations will increasingly automate data collection, analysis, and reporting processes. This automation will free up human resources for more strategic tasks and enable faster, more accurate decision-making.
2. **Greater Emphasis on Data Privacy**: As concerns about data privacy continue to rise, organizations will prioritize ethical data practices and invest in technologies that enhance data security and compliance with regulations.
3. **Enhanced Data Collaboration**: The future will see a rise in collaborative data sharing among organizations, enabling them to leverage shared insights for mutual benefit. Data partnerships will become more common, allowing organizations to combine their data for richer analysis.
4. **Focus on Real-Time Analytics**: Organizations will increasingly rely on real-time analytics to make timely decisions. The ability to analyze data as it is generated will allow organizations to respond quickly to market changes and customer needs.

5. **Integration of AI and Ethics**: As AI technologies become more prevalent, organizations will face challenges related to ethical considerations. There will be a growing need for frameworks and guidelines to ensure responsible AI use, addressing issues such as bias, transparency, and accountability.
6. **Data-Driven Innovation**: Organizations will continue to leverage data to drive innovation, using insights to develop new products, services, and business models. Data will play a pivotal role in identifying emerging trends and customer needs.

Conclusion

The future of data-driven decision-making is bright, with emerging technologies and evolving practices shaping the data landscape. As organizations embrace AI, ML, and big data, they will gain unprecedented insights to drive innovation and enhance operational efficiency. Additionally, the role of data in promoting sustainable practices will continue to grow, highlighting the importance of responsible data use. By staying informed about these trends and adapting to the changing data landscape, organizations can position themselves for success in the data-driven future. In the concluding chapter, we will summarize key takeaways and provide final thoughts on the journey toward becoming a data-driven organization.

Conclusion

As we conclude this exploration of data-driven decision-making, it is essential to reflect on the key takeaways from each chapter and consider the actionable steps organizations can take to harness the power of data effectively.

Summary of Key Takeaways

1. **The Importance of Data**: Data is a crucial asset for modern organizations, providing insights that can drive strategic decisions, enhance operational efficiency, and improve customer experiences. Embracing a data-driven culture is vital for success in today's competitive landscape.

2. **Understanding Data**: Recognizing the different types of data, their sources, and the methods for collection and management is foundational for effective data use. Organizations must be equipped to differentiate between quantitative and qualitative data and know how to gather insights from both.

3. **Data Analysis Techniques**: A variety of data analysis techniques—descriptive, diagnostic, predictive, and prescriptive—can be employed to extract valuable insights. Utilizing the right tools and software is critical for effective data analysis.

4. **Frameworks for Decision-Making**: Incorporating structured frameworks like the OODA Loop and SWOT analysis can help organizations integrate data insights into their strategic planning processes, ensuring that decisions are informed by accurate data.

5. **Learning from Case Studies**: Analyzing successful implementations and failures provides invaluable lessons. Organizations can learn from the strategies that propelled companies like Amazon and Netflix to success, as well as the pitfalls faced by others like Blockbuster and Yahoo.

6. **Building a Data-Driven Culture**: Leadership support, employee training, and interdepartmental collaboration are essential for fostering a culture that values data-driven decision-making. Organizations must prioritize these elements to empower their workforce.

7. **Ethical Considerations**: Navigating ethical considerations in data use is paramount. Organizations must address privacy concerns, minimize bias in data and decision-making, and ensure compliance with relevant regulations to maintain trust and accountability.

8. **Future Trends**: Emerging technologies, including AI, ML, and big data, are shaping the future of data-driven decision-making. Organizations must stay ahead of these trends and adapt to the evolving data landscape while emphasizing sustainable practices and ethical data use.

Call to Action for Organizations

Organizations today stand at a pivotal moment where the ability to leverage data effectively can distinguish them from competitors and drive sustainable growth. As you embark on your journey toward becoming a data-driven organization, consider the following actions:

1. **Invest in Data Literacy**: Provide ongoing training and development opportunities to enhance the data literacy of your workforce. Empower employees to analyze and interpret data confidently.
2. **Cultivate Leadership Commitment**: Ensure that leadership actively supports data-driven initiatives and fosters a culture that prioritizes data in decision-making processes.
3. **Implement Ethical Frameworks**: Establish ethical guidelines and frameworks for data use to address privacy concerns and bias. Prioritize transparency and accountability in all data practices.
4. **Embrace Emerging Technologies**: Stay informed about emerging technologies and trends in data analytics. Evaluate and adopt tools that can enhance your organization's data capabilities.
5. **Foster Collaboration**: Encourage collaboration across departments to break down silos and promote the sharing of data insights. Create cross-functional teams that leverage diverse perspectives.

6. **Focus on Sustainability**: Use data to drive sustainable practices within your organization. Analyze resource usage and supply chain practices to minimize environmental impact and promote social responsibility.
7. **Adapt and Innovate**: Be agile in adapting to changing market dynamics and evolving customer needs. Use data-driven insights to innovate and refine your products, services, and business strategies.

By embracing these actions, organizations can unlock the full potential of data-driven decision-making, positioning themselves for long-term success in an increasingly data-centric world. The journey toward becoming a data-driven organization is ongoing, but the rewards—improved efficiency, enhanced customer experiences, and sustainable growth—are well worth the effort.

Additional Components

Appendices

Appendix A: Glossary of Terms

1. **Big Data**: Large and complex data sets that traditional data processing applications cannot handle. Often characterized by the three Vs: Volume, Velocity, and Variety.
2. **Data Analytics**: The process of examining data sets to conclude the information they contain, often using specialized software and techniques.

3. **Data Governance**: The management of data availability, usability, integrity, and security within an organization.
4. **Data Mining**: The practice of analyzing large data sets to uncover patterns and extract valuable insights.
5. **Descriptive Analysis**: A method of data analysis that focuses on summarizing historical data to understand trends and patterns.
6. **Machine Learning (ML)**: A subset of artificial intelligence that enables systems to learn from data and improve their performance over time without explicit programming.
7. **Predictive Analysis**: Techniques that use statistical algorithms and machine learning to identify the likelihood of future outcomes based on historical data.
8. **Prescriptive Analysis**: A form of data analysis that provides recommendations for actions based on predictive outcomes.
9. **Structured Data**: Data that is organized in a predefined manner, making it easily searchable and analyzable (e.g., databases).
10. **Unstructured Data**: Data that does not have a predefined format, making it more challenging to analyze (e.g., text, images).

Appendix B: Recommended Tools and Resources

1. **Data Analysis Tools**:
    - **Microsoft Excel**: Widely used for data analysis and visualization.
    - **Tableau**: A powerful data visualization tool that helps convert data into interactive and shareable dashboards.

- **R and Python**: Programming languages with extensive libraries for data analysis and machine learning.

2. **Data Management Solutions**:
   - **SQL Server**: A relational database management system for storing and retrieving data.
   - **MongoDB**: A NoSQL database that allows for flexible data storage and real-time analytics.
   - **Apache Hadoop**: A framework for processing large data sets across distributed computing environments.

3. **Machine Learning Platforms**:
   - **Google Cloud AI**: Offers machine learning tools and APIs for building and deploying models.
   - **IBM Watson**: Provides a suite of AI tools and solutions for businesses.
   - **AWS SageMaker**: A platform for building, training, and deploying machine learning models.

4. **Ethics and Compliance Resources**:
   - **General Data Protection Regulation (GDPR)**: Guidelines for data protection and privacy in the European Union.
   - **California Consumer Privacy Act (CCPA)**: A state statute that enhances privacy rights for residents of California.
   - **Data Protection Officer Resources**: Organizations can refer to various guidelines and best practices for appointing and training DPOs.

5. **Online Courses and Certifications**:

- **Coursera**: Offers a variety of data science and analytics courses from leading universities.
- **edX**: Provides online courses on data analysis, machine learning, and data ethics.
- **Udacity**: Features nano degree programs in data science, AI, and machine learning.

References and Further Reading

1. **Books**:
    - Davenport, T. H., & Harris, J. G. (2007). *Competing on Analytics: The New Science of Winning*. Harvard Business Review Press.
    - Hilbert, M., & López, P. (2011). *The World's Technological Capacity to Store, Communicate and Compute Information*. Science, 332(6025), 60-65.
    - Provost, F., & Fawcett, T. (2013). *Data Science for Business: What You Need to Know about Data Mining and Data-Analytic Thinking*. O'Reilly Media.
2. **Articles**:
    - Marr, B. (2018). *How Data Science is Changing Business*. Forbes. Retrieved from Forbes.
    - Kelleher, J. D., & Tierney, B. (2018). *Data Science: A Practical Introduction to Programming and Data Analysis*. The MIT Press.
3. **Online Resources**:
    - Data Science Central: A community for data science professionals to share insights and resources.

- Towards Data Science: A Medium publication offering articles and tutorials on data science topics.
- KDnuggets: A leading site on AI, data science, machine learning, and analytics.

- **Regulatory Resources**:
  - European Commission. (2018). *General Data Protection Regulation (GDPR)*. Retrieved from European Commission.
  - California Department of Justice. (2020). *California Consumer Privacy Act (CCPA)*. Retrieved from California DOJ.

www.ingramcontent.com/pod-product-compliance
Lightning Source LLC
Chambersburg PA
CBHW070420230526
45471CB00006B/2897